All's Fair in Love & War
The Ultimate Cartoon Book
by the
World's Greatest Cartoonists

All's Fair in Love & War

THE ULTIMATE CARTOON BOOK

by the

World's Greatest Cartoonists

———

Bob Eckstein, editor

PRINCETON ARCHITECTURAL PRESS · NEW YORK

Introduction

On his TV show *Adam Ruins Everything*, comedian Adam Conover makes a compelling case for celebrating reaching the ten-year mark in a marriage that ends in divorce, reasoning that being with one person for that long deserves a certificate of merit and, anyway, is the most to be expected. Love is hard.

At least divorce has gotten easier. "In the old days, if you wanted a divorce, you needed to establish that one person was entirely at fault, and the other was totally innocent," writes Stephanie Coontz in *Marriage, a History*.

Divorce today? It's easy peasy, as in Victoria Roberts's cartoon (page 84) of a wife with her luggage announcing to her husband, "It's National We're History Month."

This book might have been titled *How To Be Happily Married*, but there were already about fourteen books with that title. I contend that this book is funnier than all of them—and more helpful. As the wife's lover hiding in a closet pointing to a pie chart in Sam Gross's cartoon (page 11) tells the husband: "I can explain everything."

Studies show humor is an important component in any successful relationship and in finding love. Humor is a primary sexual attractor for partners seeking a mate, perhaps because one's comic chops are a demonstration of intelligence.

I have found, personally, that having a solid five or ten minutes of good material is crucial in finding a mate. Your love isn't really tested until after the object of your desire has heard all your stories. For most of us that's about four weeks, five tops. And maybe that's the real reason so many of us get divorced—one of the two parties has simply run out of interesting things to say.

Love certainly is a many-splendored thing, and a royal pain in the ass. I myself have never found love to be easy. Instead of love at first sight, my experience was more like that of cartoonist Warren Miller's Sisyphus pushing the world's largest "Be My Valentine" Sweethearts candy up a hill (page 14). In my case, there was a college classmate who despised me. A dozen years later I ran into this enemy at a funeral. Because nothing in life makes any sense, and maybe in the spirit of dark humor, we decided, in short time, to elope. So, two takeaways: 1) While it may seem from this collection that the common progression is love, marriage, divorce, actually, never rule out hate, marriage, love; and 2) funerals can be meat markets. Everyone is vulnerable, and wearing black is very slimming. Consider one of comedy's most famous lines: "Too soon?"

I don't expect everyone to marry their school-days enemy, but the heart wants what the heart wants. All I really know is that I love all the cartoons in this collection. Once again, I have called upon the best and wisest cartoonists to share their thoughts on the subject of love and marriage, and their responses, I assure you, will surprise and delight. Only the very funniest and the most attractive cartoons wooed me over. I'm convinced there is more to learn on the ways of love in this book than in any study out there. Humor is the world's greatest aphrodisiac—I suspect all these cartoonists are getting laid a lot.

—*Bob Eckstein*

"I can't believe he brought her."

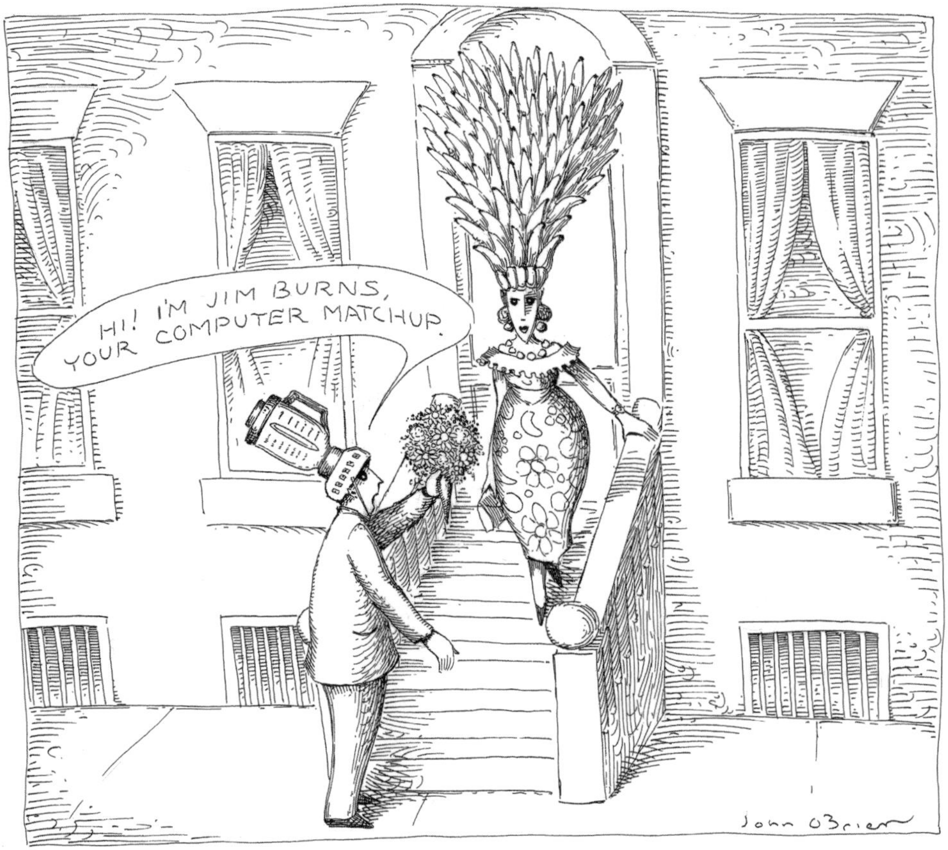
HI! I'M JIM BURNS, YOUR COMPUTER MATCHUP.
John O'Brien

"Why, Mr. Conly, I do believe you're trying to get me hydrated."

"Let's do this, let's fall in love."

"I can explain everything."

JUST MARRIED
SORRY WE DIDN'T INVITE YOU, IT WAS A SMALL WEDDING.

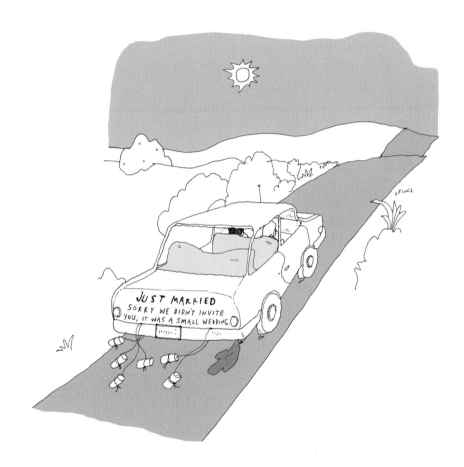

"You're really nice, Richard. I was hoping I could fix you up with my mom."

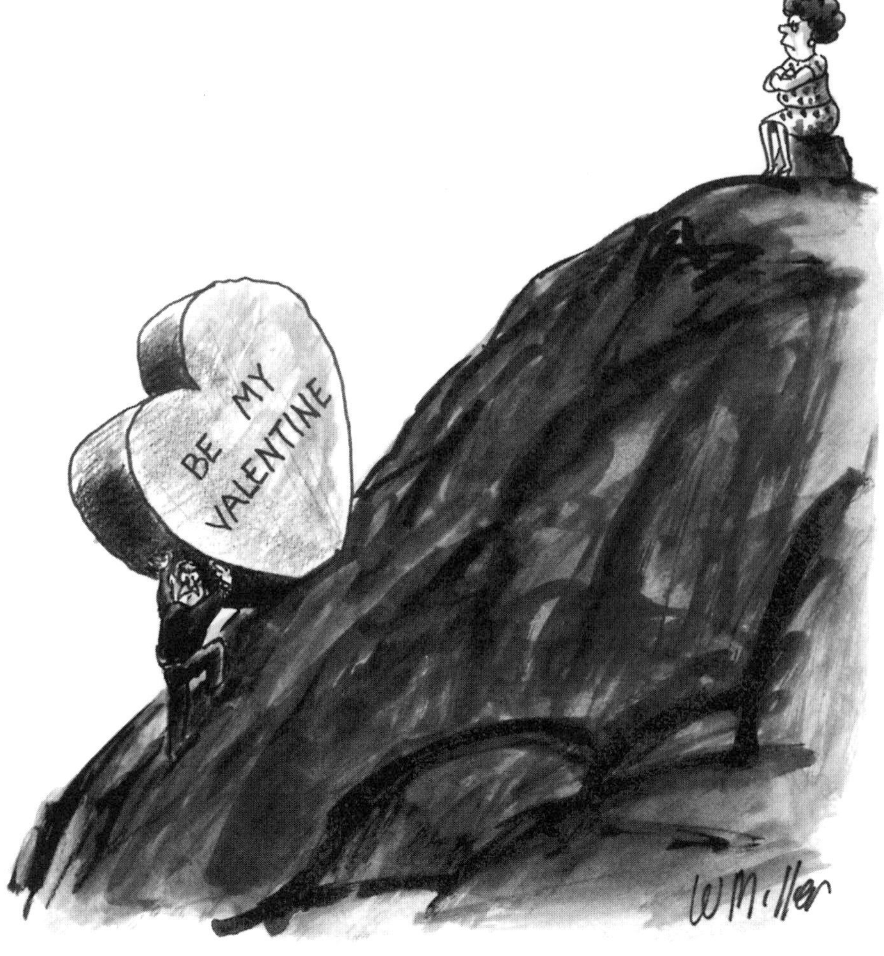
BE MY VALENTINE
W Miller

"So I'm told we were once married. Can you tell us what that was like?"

"Gays and lesbians getting married—haven't they suffered enough?"

"That's two of each, including Noah and his girlfriend."

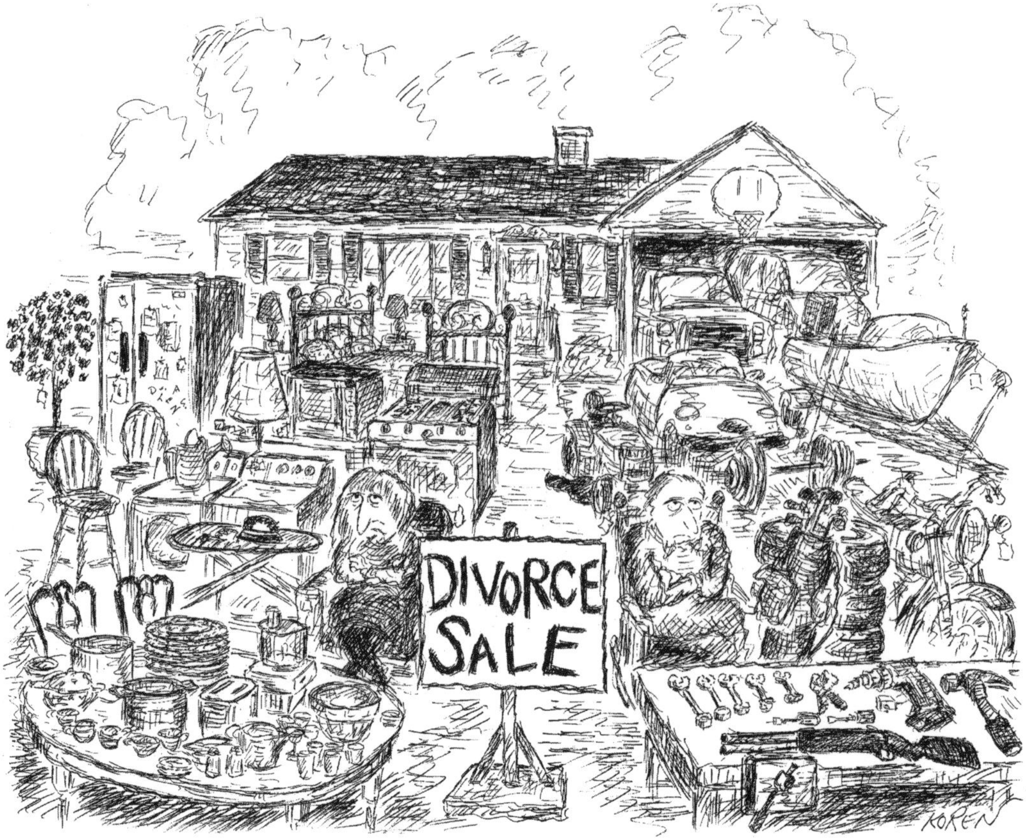
DIVORCE
SALE
KOREN

"Since we don't have children, my ex turned the cats against me."

"Those were all my husbands. No two were exactly alike."

"I know that's you, Susan."

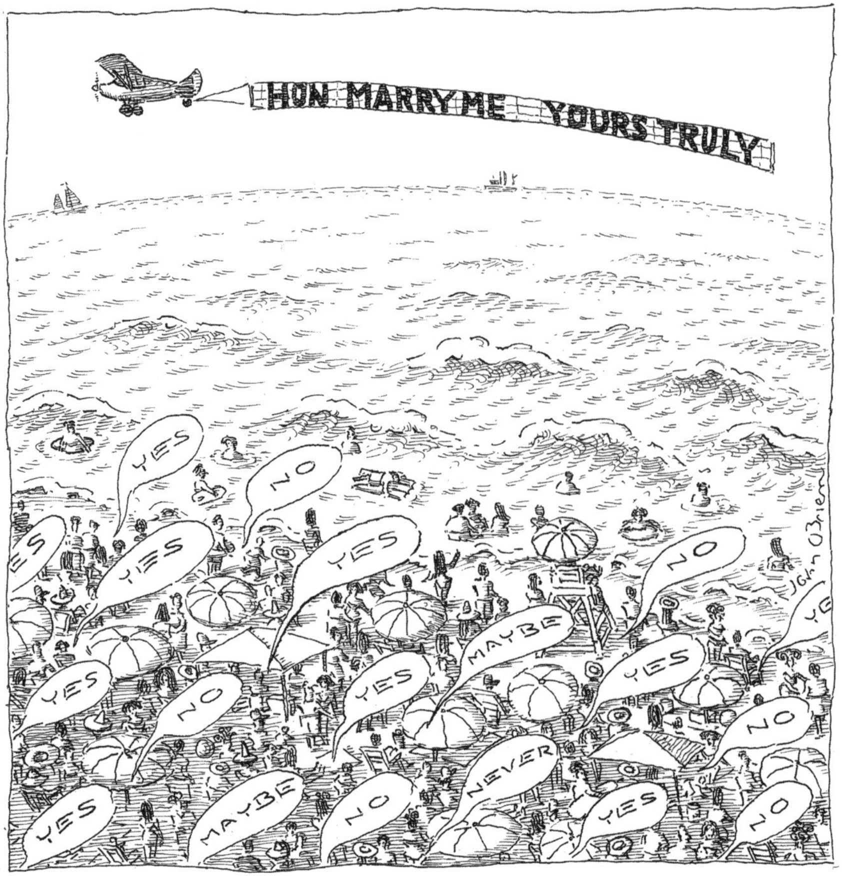
HON MARRY ME YOURS TRULY
YES
NO
YES
YES
NO
YES
YES
NO
MAYBE
YES
YES
NO
YES
NO
MAYBE
NO
NEVER
YES
NO
John O'Brien

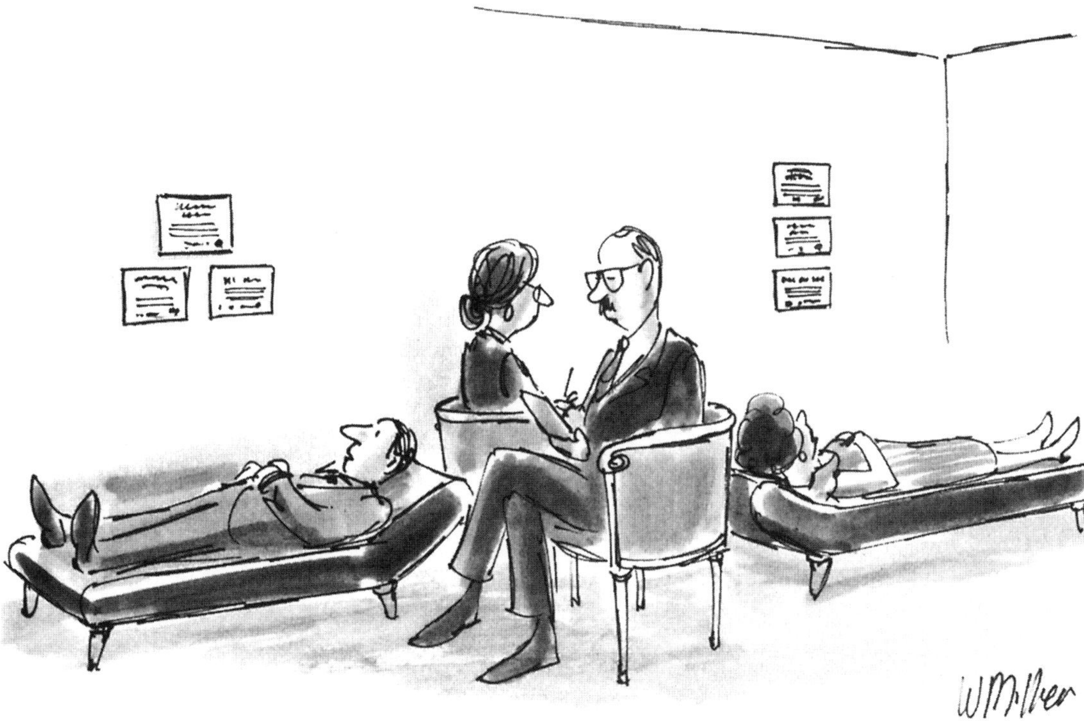
WMiller

"When I was a little girl, I always dreamed of a big divorce."

"No, no, no—stay as late as you want. In fact, divorce me."

"My parents completely accept you as family. They just don't like you."

"Right now I'm between drinks."

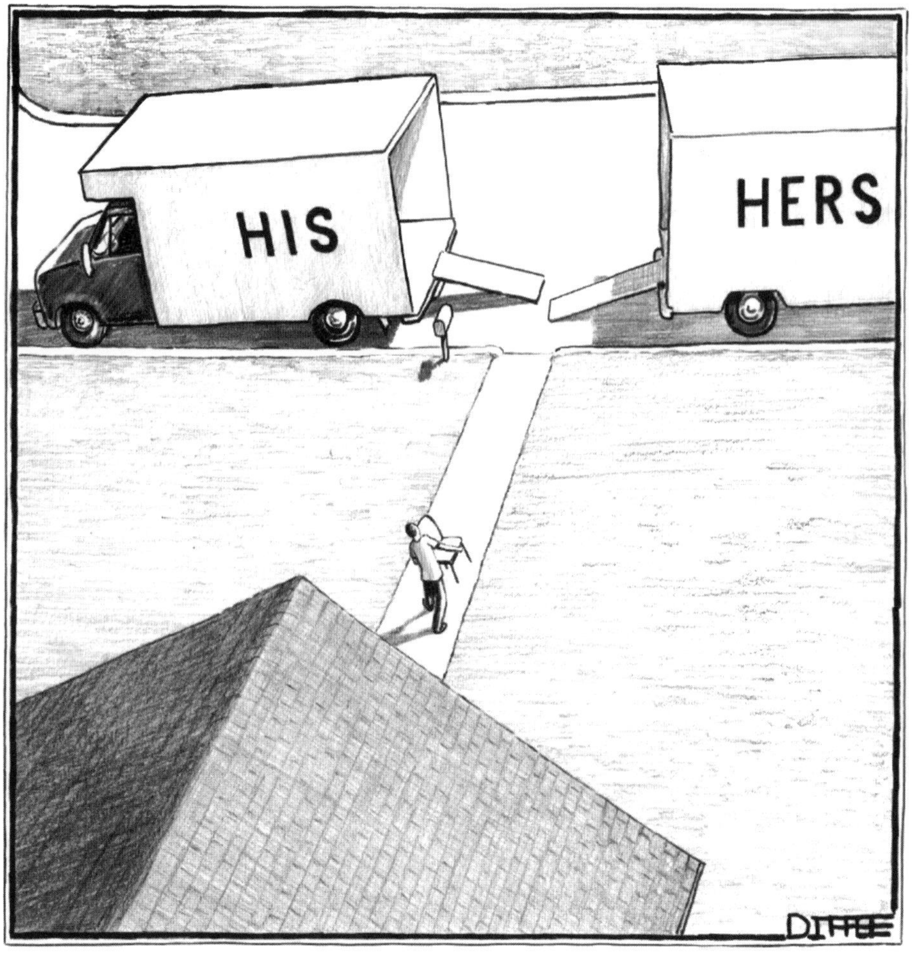
HIS
HERS
DIFFEE

"My wife doesn't understand me, especially when she gets wind of situations like this."

"You'd save a world of fuss by not shootin' at me in the first place."

"It's been too long, I can't remember the last time we all got together as a group and had sex."

"Look, until there's a Tinder for pandas, we have to meet the old-fashioned way: being locked in a room together by scientists."

"My wife doesn't understand me."

"You always take the parking spot of least resistance."

"I thought you'd be happy that I was finally getting some exercise."

"Your father and I want to explain why we've decided to live apart."

"Sorry—I thought this was your brother's room."

"I'm just not sure if I want to bring a child into this crazy, messed-up world."

"I'm having my wedding ring melted down into a bullet."

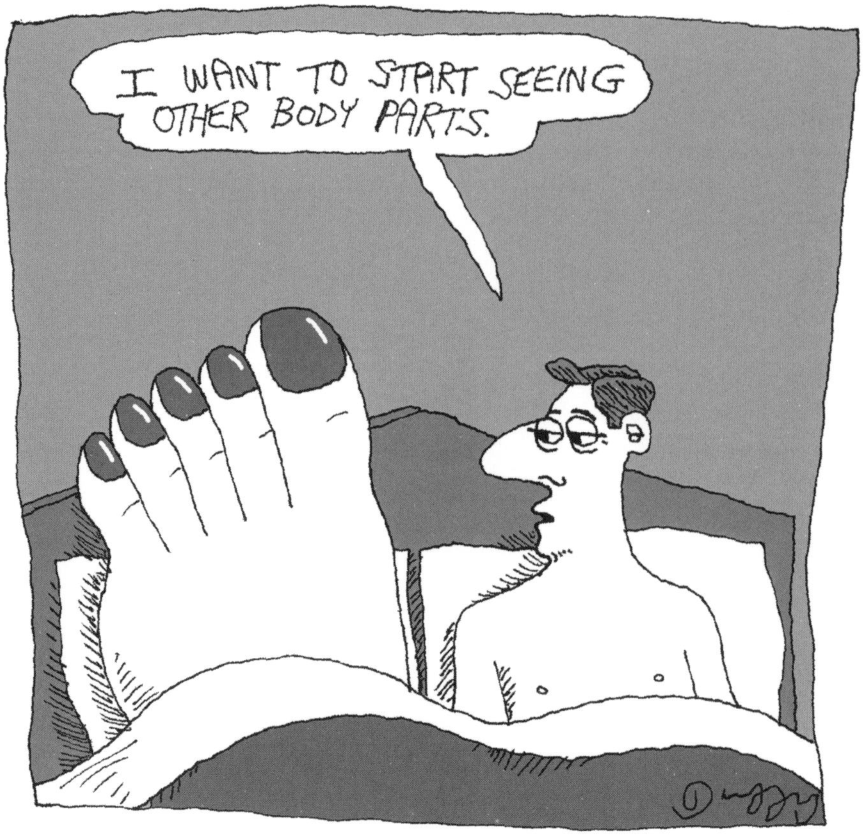
I WANT TO START SEEING OTHER BODY PARTS.

"But that's enough about me. Tell me, what do you do?"

"We met in Milwaukee."

"Play that one you played when we first met and I thought
there was something definitely wrong with you."

"For heaven's sake, Melissa, she's my mother. I can't tell her to leave."

"At first he only wore them leaf blowing—now he wears them all the time."

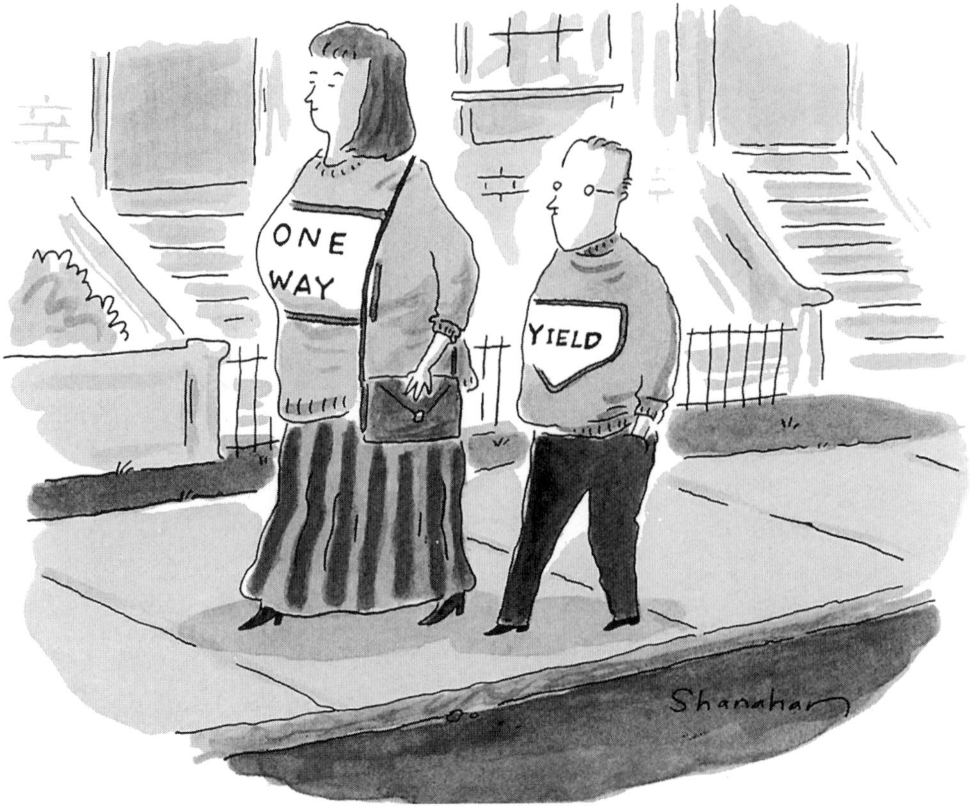
ONE WAY
YIELD
Shanahan

"Good morning, folks, this is Captain Holwood from the flight deck.
We'll be cruising at thirty-five thousand feet today, and I'll be finally taking control
of my life, struggling to satisfy the needs of only one person—me!"

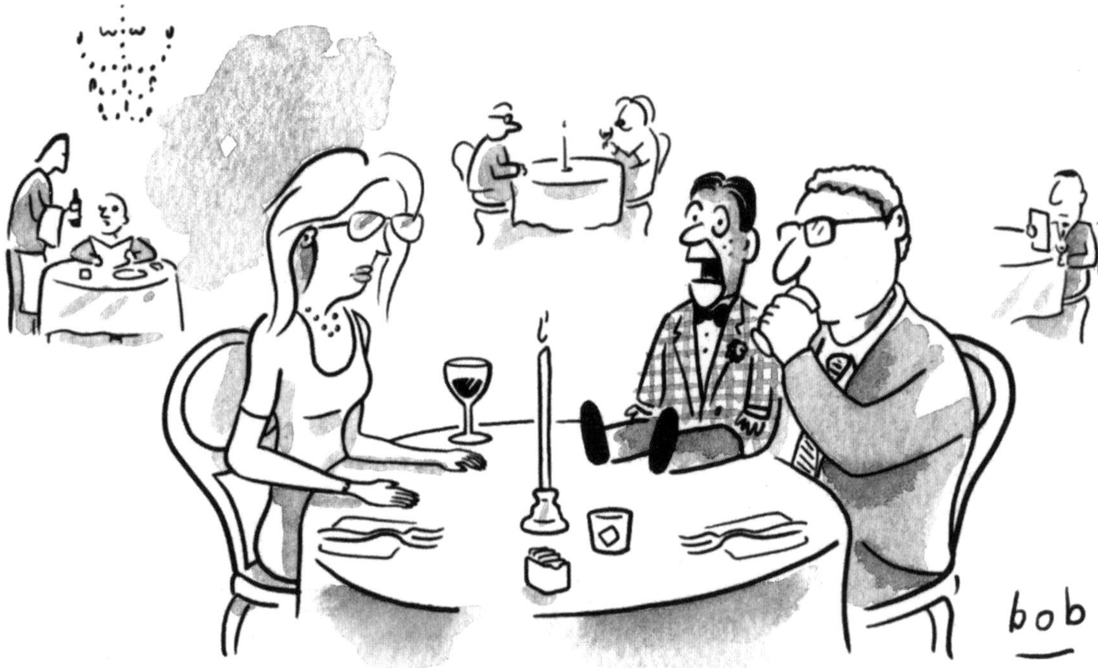
bob

"It's not you, it's him."

"Why don't you try one before you start comparing them to oranges?"

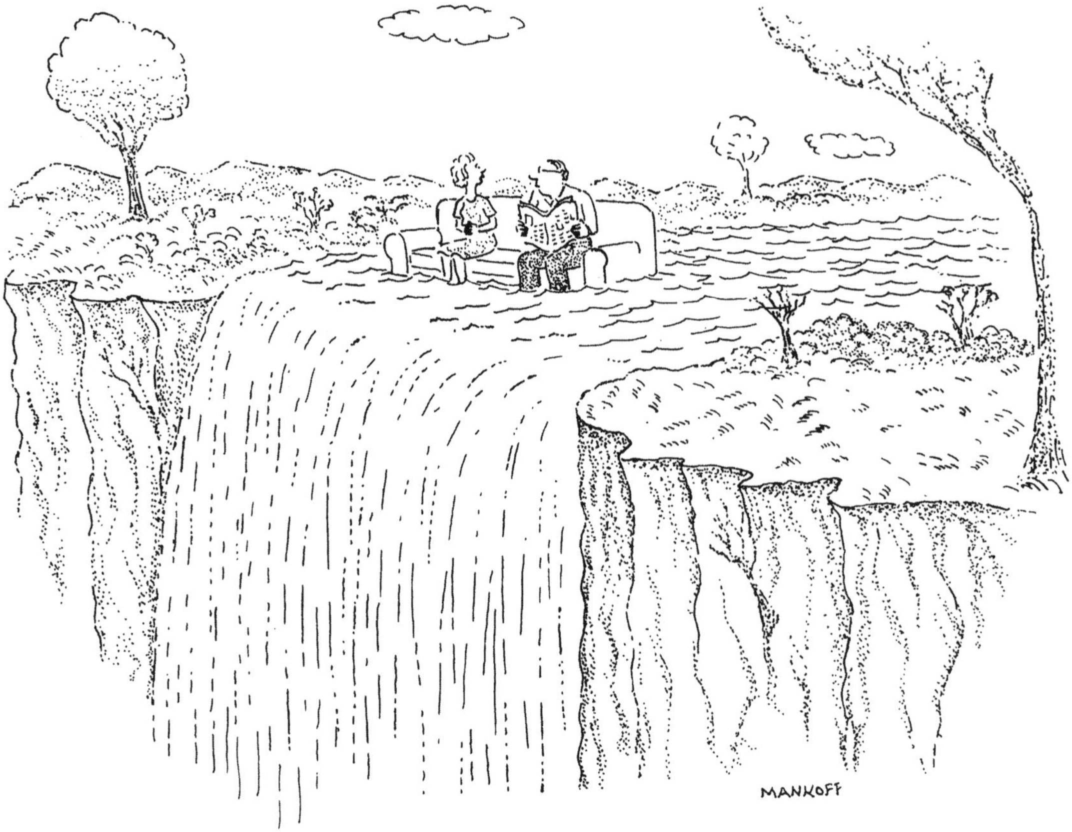
MANKOFF

"Brad, we've got to talk."

"His wife and family will decide on the course of treatment, but, as his ex, feel free to open up a few old wounds."

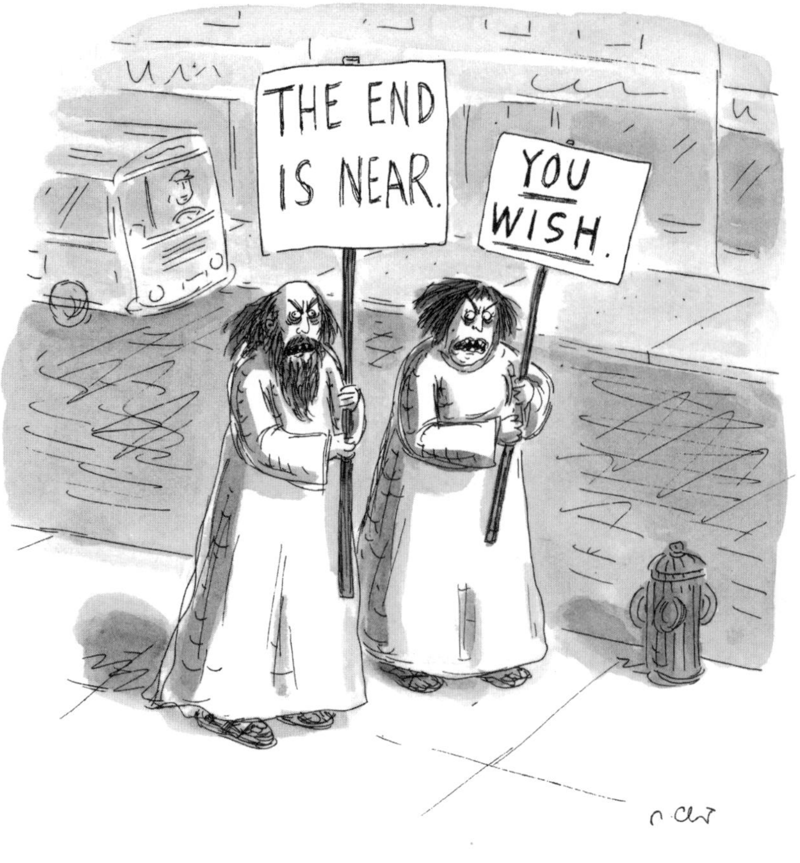
THE END IS NEAR.
YOU WISH.

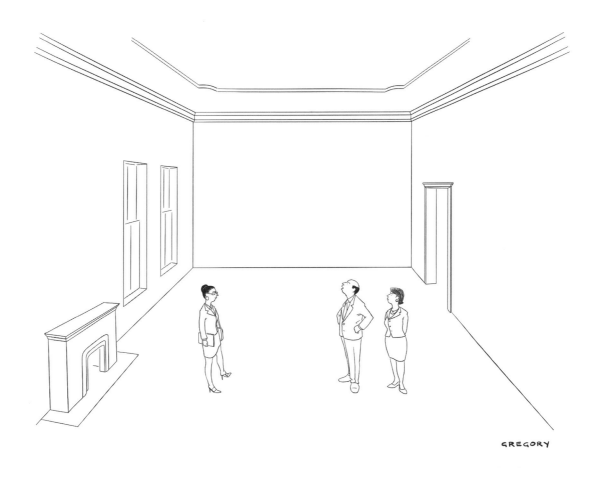

"Wow…we could really fill this room with uncomfortable silences."

"Say, that bald gentleman over there. Do you know if he's married or seeing anyone?"

"Why do we need some piece of paper to say that we hate each other?"

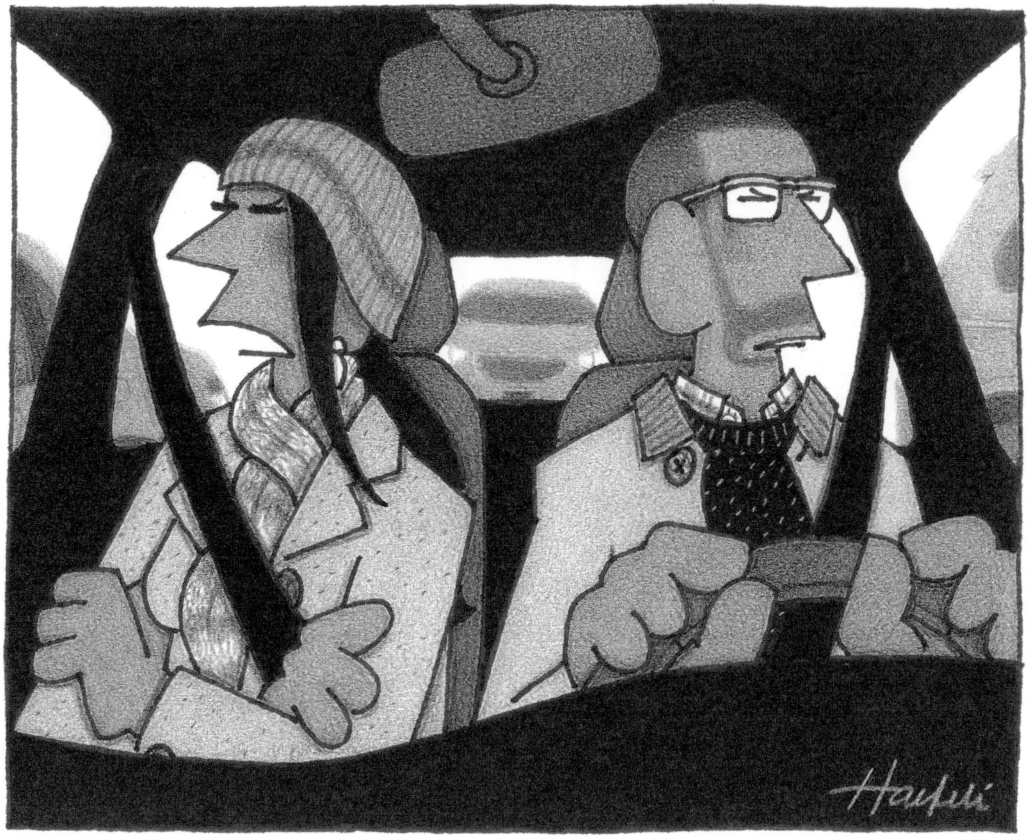
Haefeli

"You seem to have no trouble committing when it comes to a lane on the highway."

"My client doesn't have to answer that."

"I think we should see other species."

"I don't care if she is a tape dispenser. I love her."

"I see here the party of the first part says 'potato.' The party of the second part says 'potahto.'
The party of the first part says 'tomato,' the party of the second part says 'tomahto.'
Both parties, by mutual agreement, wish to call the whole thing off."

"Sometimes I think you only married me for the political statement."

MRS. TAMBOURINE MAN

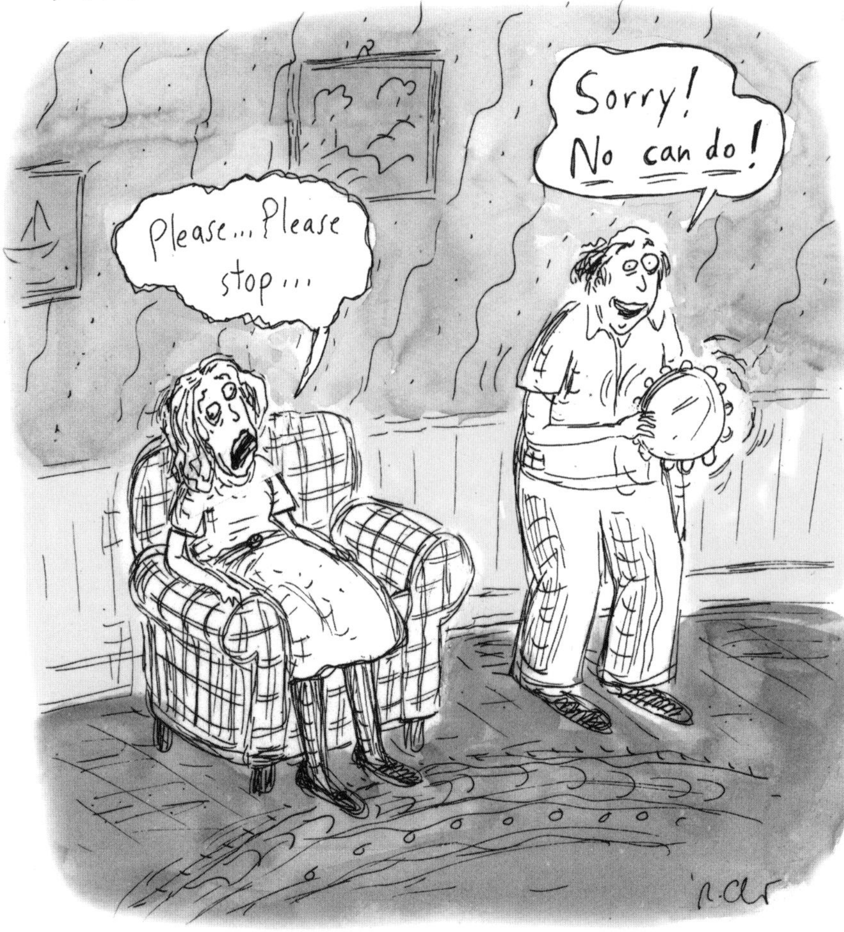

"Helen! Well, I'll be damned."

"I've become so good at dating, relationships that
used to take months now last a matter of days."

"I followed your husband yesterday. He spent the whole day following you."

"Ok. How about I throw in a necklace, too?"

"It's not just that he walks upright and uses complex tools. He also makes me laugh."

"I know. But I think I can change him."

"In my family we say 'I love you' all the time. The words have lost all meaning."

"Or, on the count of three, we could just kiss and make up."

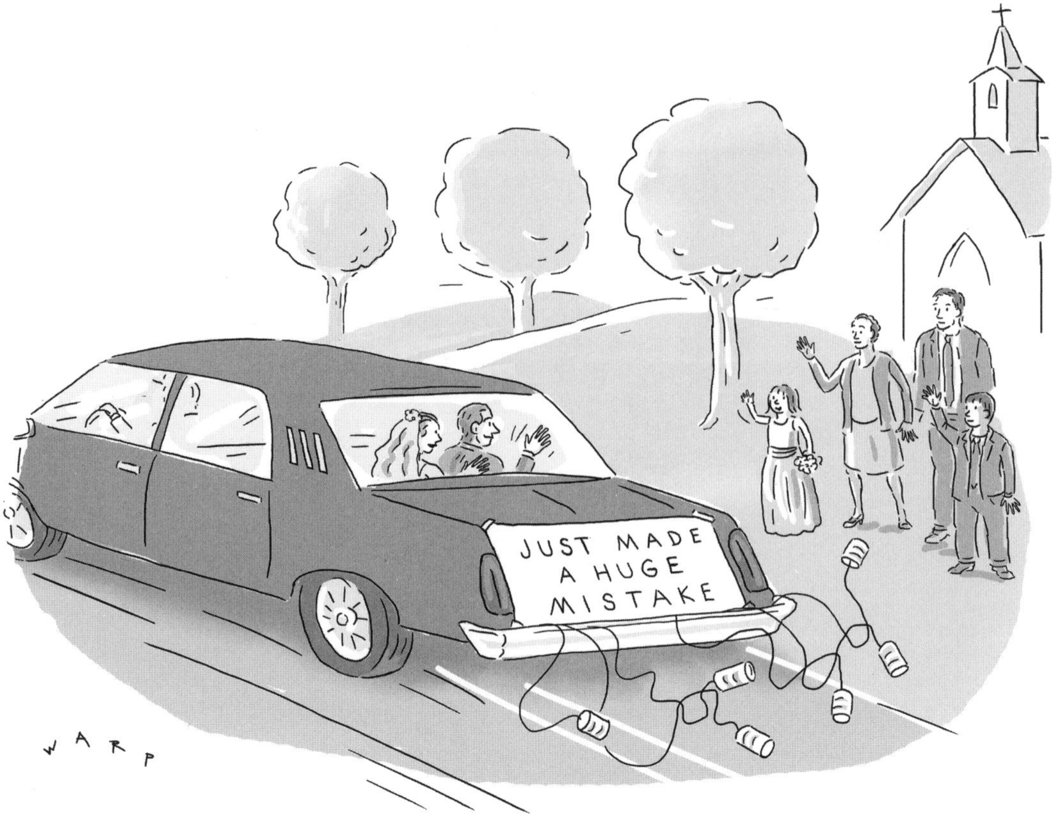
JUST MADE
A HUGE
MISTAKE
WARP

"I've never felt like this on a first date, Tom, but you're suffocating me."

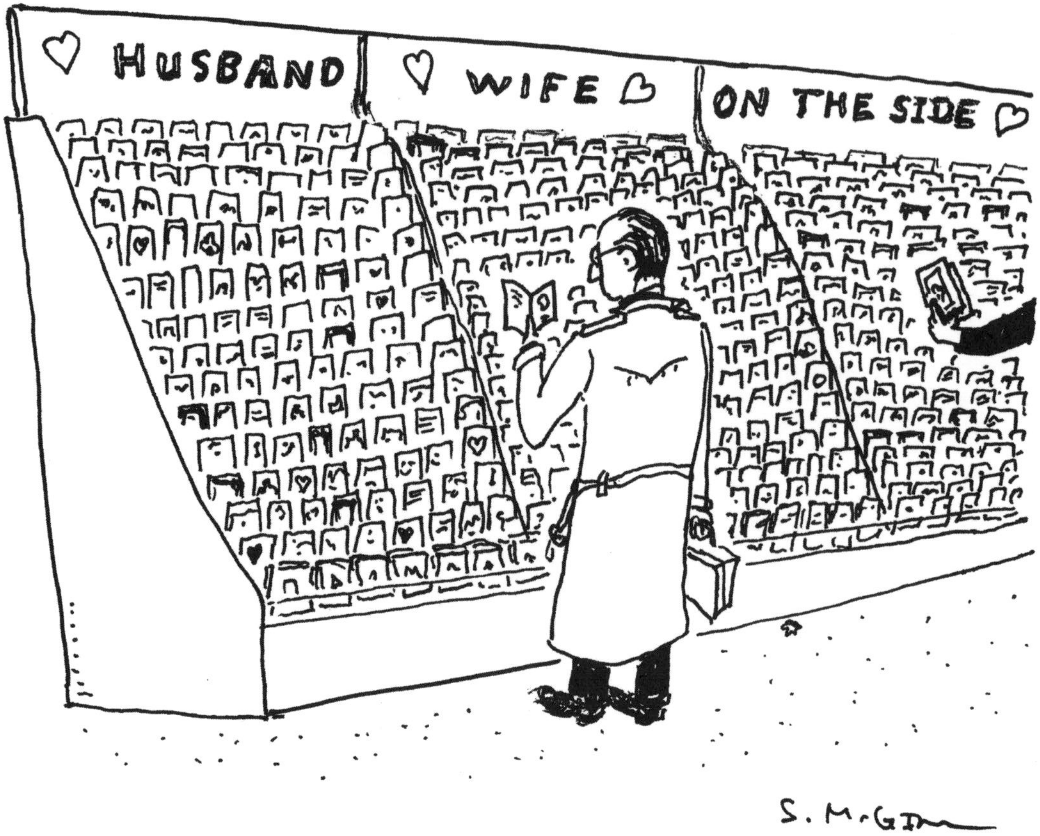
HUSBAND
WIFE
ON THE SIDE
S. McGINN

"He's cute but not equality-for-marriage-under-the-law cute."

"Ms. Palmer will marry you now."

"When we were together, he was always singing 'It Had to Be You.'
Then, suddenly, he switched to 'I Gotta Be Me,' and I haven't seen him since."

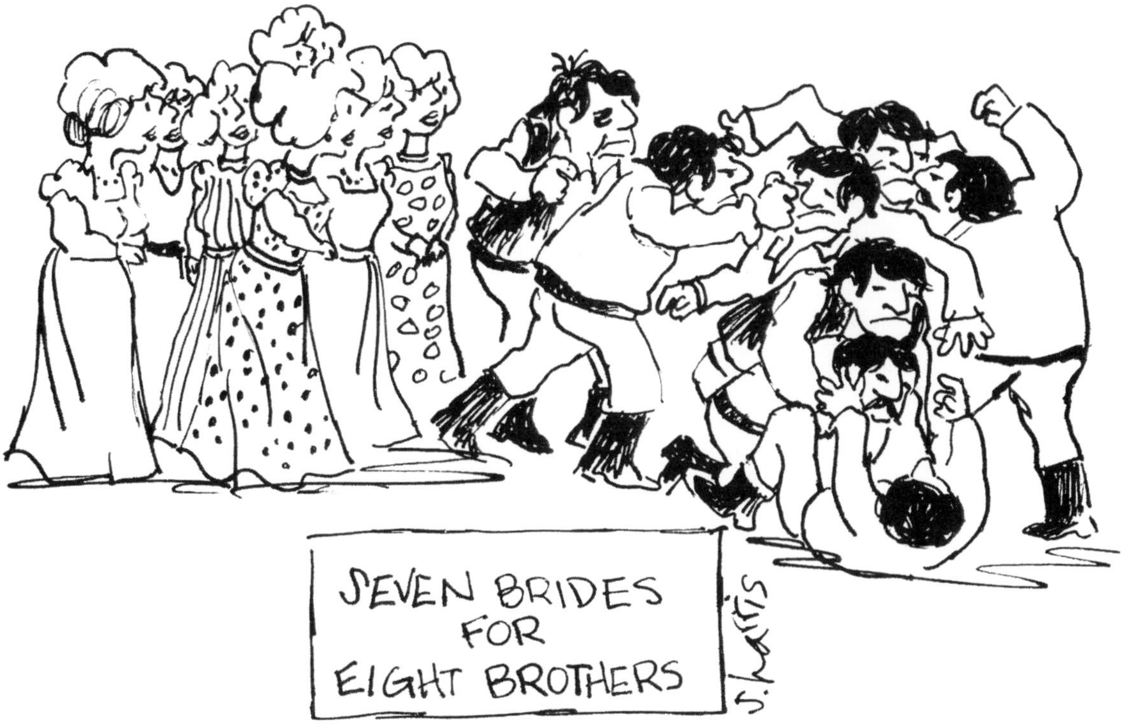
SEVEN BRIDES
FOR
EIGHT BROTHERS

"Whoa, someone's been doing some gathering."

"Remember, you're under oath."

"The only thing we didn't plan on was falling in love."

"I went to farmers' markets with my first wife.
I don't know if I want to go through all that again."

"Mother was right about you. You're a toaster."

"It's National We're History Month."

"We'll always have Plaster of Paris."

"It's like you haven't heard a single word I've thought."

"Why are all the guys I meet either married, gay, or undead?"

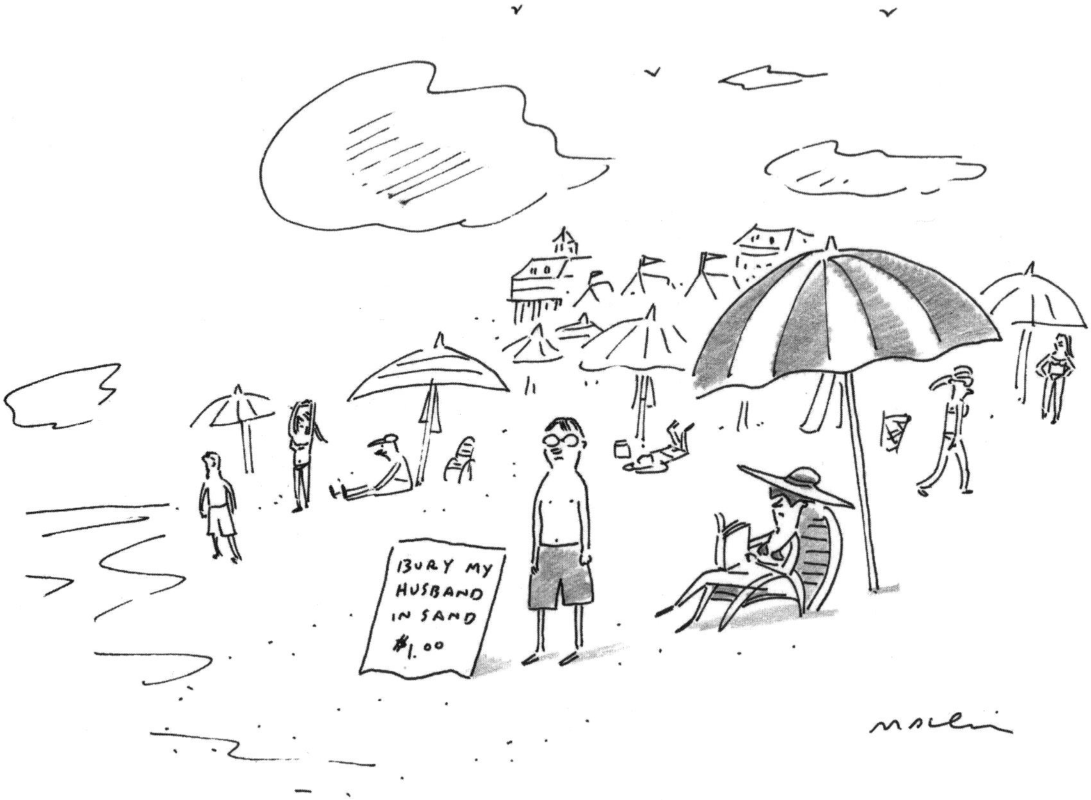
BURY MY
HUSBAND
IN SAND
$1.00

"Is there an ex-wife somewhere in there?"

"Before you go, would you mind taking a few moments
to fill out a short form rating your relationship experience?"

"You should go sit out in the sun. Get some color. You'd look good with a tan.
And a cigarette. I think you'd look really good with a tan and a cigarette."

"Two words: nude housework."

"I really shouldn't have any dessert. My trainer told me never to eat out of boredom."

LONG DISTANCE RELATIONSHIP

"Your mother and I are separating because
I want what's best for the country and your mother doesn't."

"Can you recommend something for the attorney who got me everything?"

"Take a shower first. You smell like a chimney."

"I want you to be able to feel that you can hide anything from me."

"We've been married for 5 years—which is 205 in celebrity years."

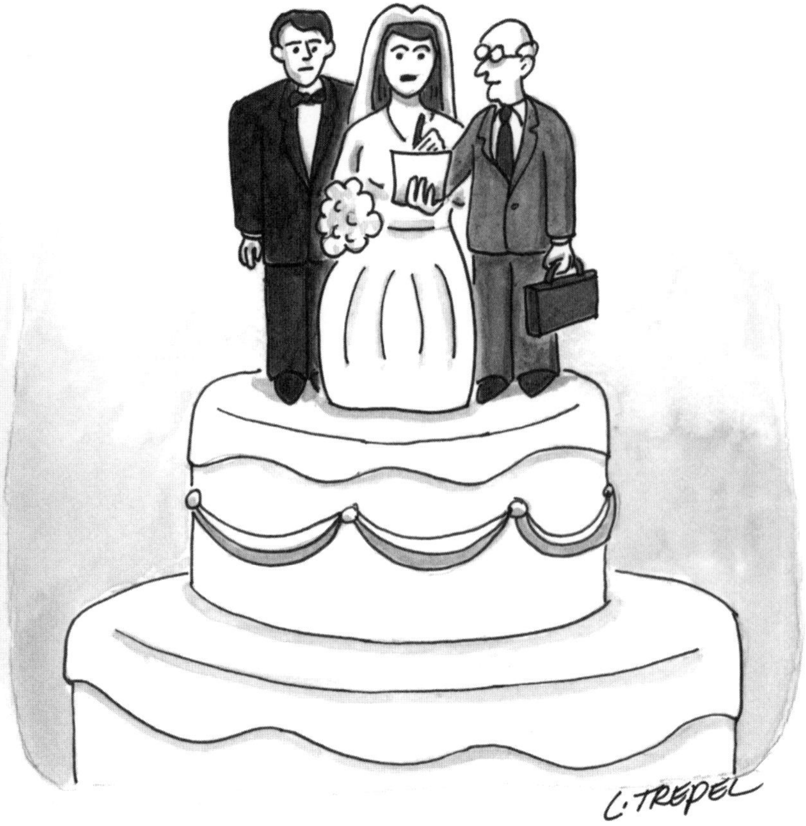
L. TREPEL

"Of all the wet cement, in all the towns, in all the worlds, she walks into mine."

"I got the kids, but he got the nanny."

"Oh, Josh is not my husband. He's my acting husband."

"I'm leaving you, Henry, and I'm taking the cat."

"And now here's Nancy with an alternate version of that very same story."

"Do these abs make me look gay?"

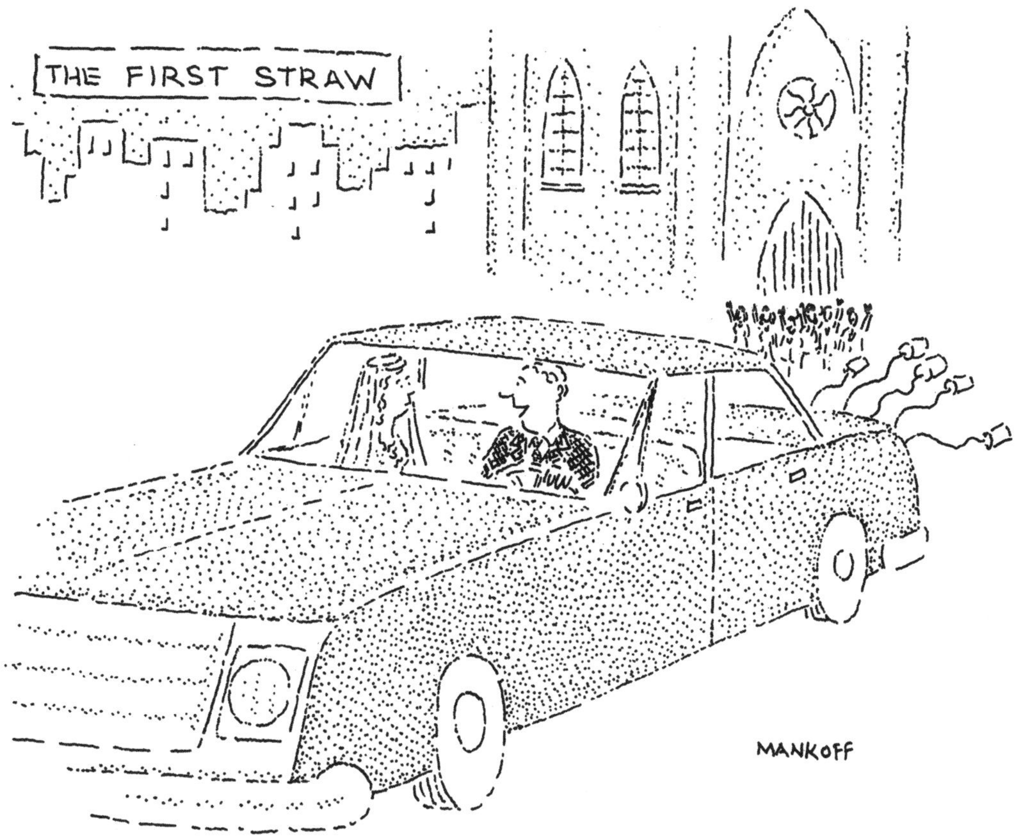
THE FIRST STRAW
MANKOFF

"Mind if I put on the game?"

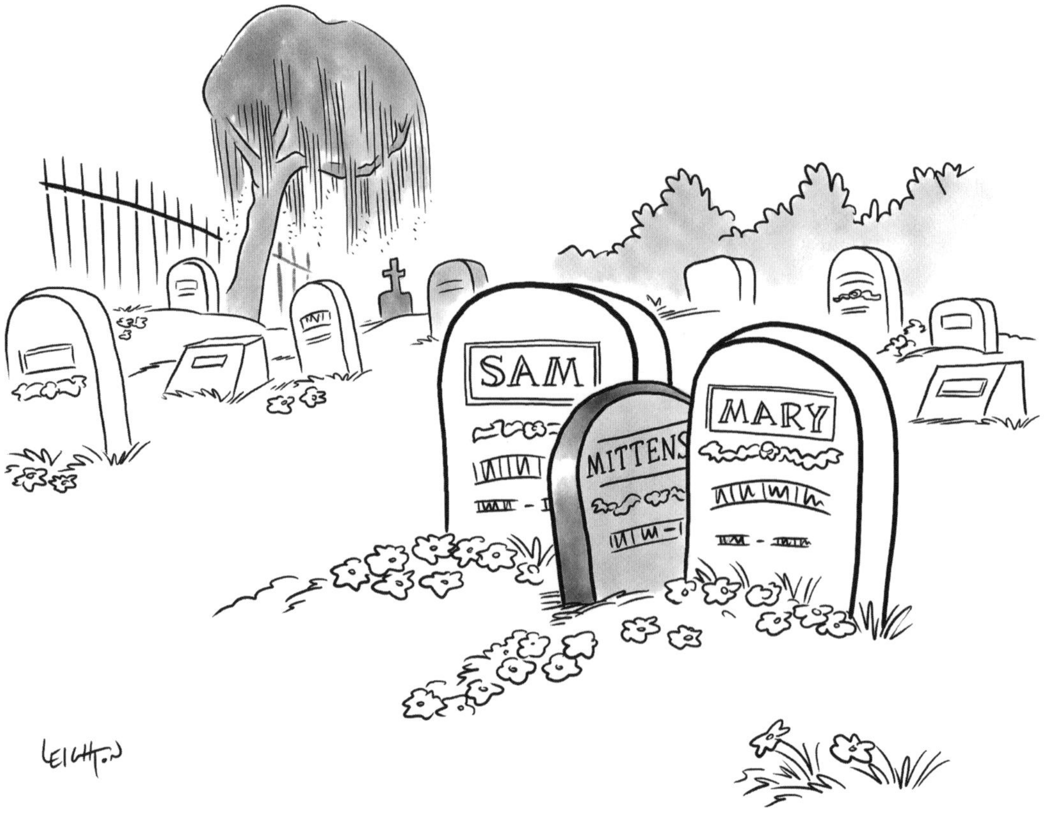
SAM
MITTENS
MARY
LEIGHTON

"You and I are just too different. You say 'tomato' and
I'm sleeping with your best friend Marcus."

"I do not have a roving eye. I have attention-deficit disorder."

"Come ON, Doris. You need to stop deluding yourself
and telling everyone that I got lost! I left! I. LEFT."

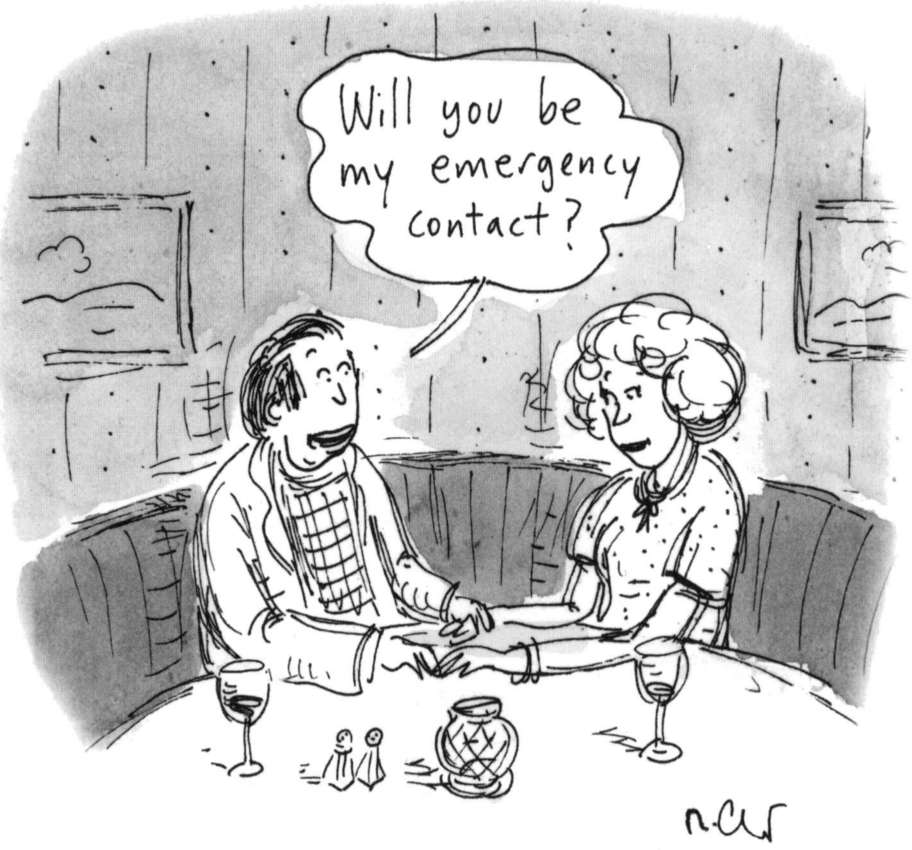
Will you be my emergency contact?

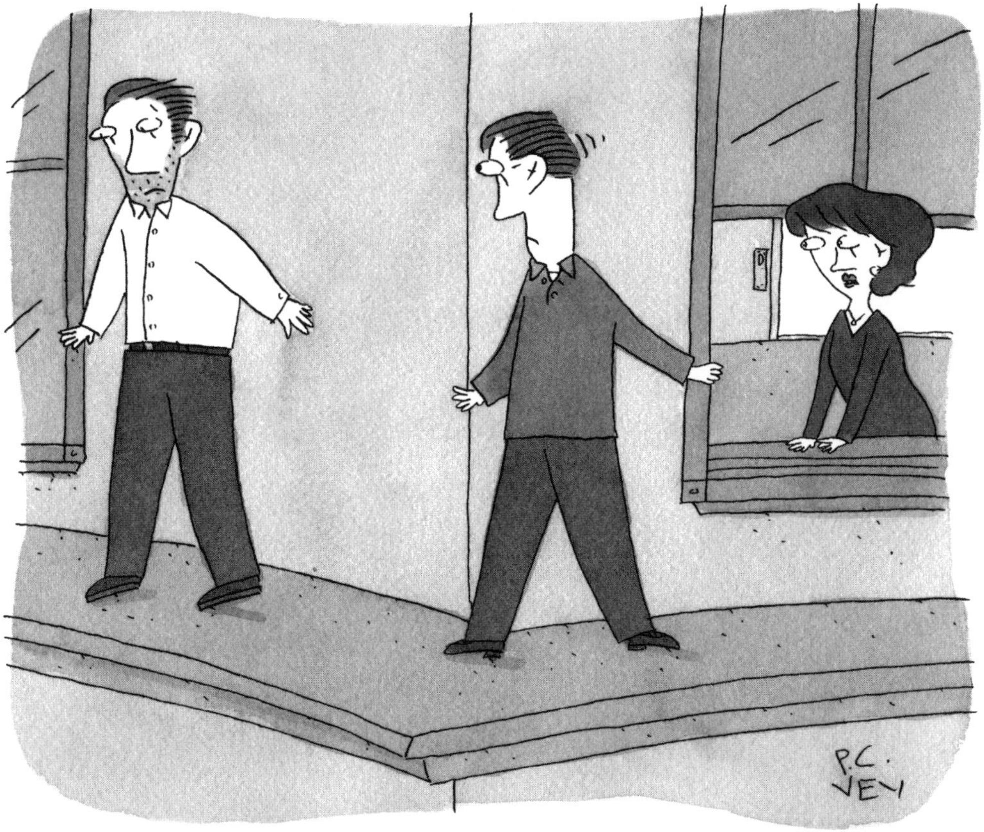
P.C.
VEY

"Him? Oh, just a friend."

"Wake up, Harold—you're dreaming again."

"Relax, Harold—now *I'm* dreaming."

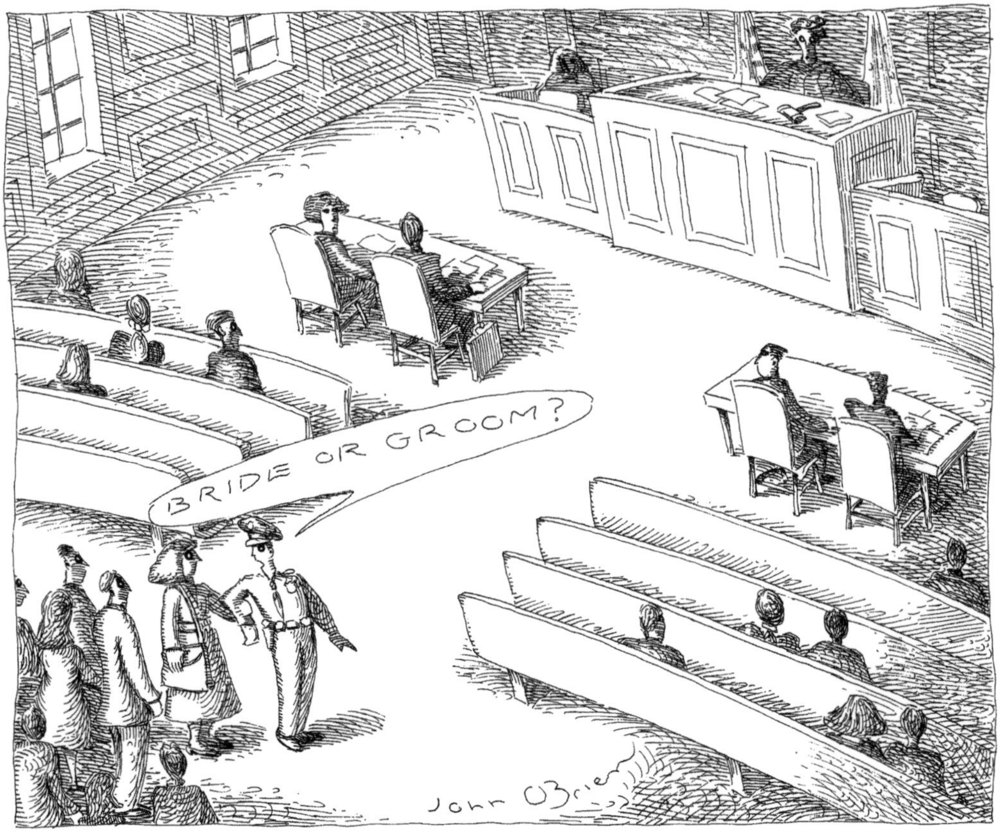
BRIDE OR GROOM?
John O'Brien

"I told you coming to your ex-wife's wedding was a mistake."

"I have something to tell you when you get back."

"Stop referring to you and me as 'we'!"

SPOCK & KIRK - THE FINAL FRONTIER.

"I honestly don't know what you're waiting for.
By the time I was your age, I'd been married twice."

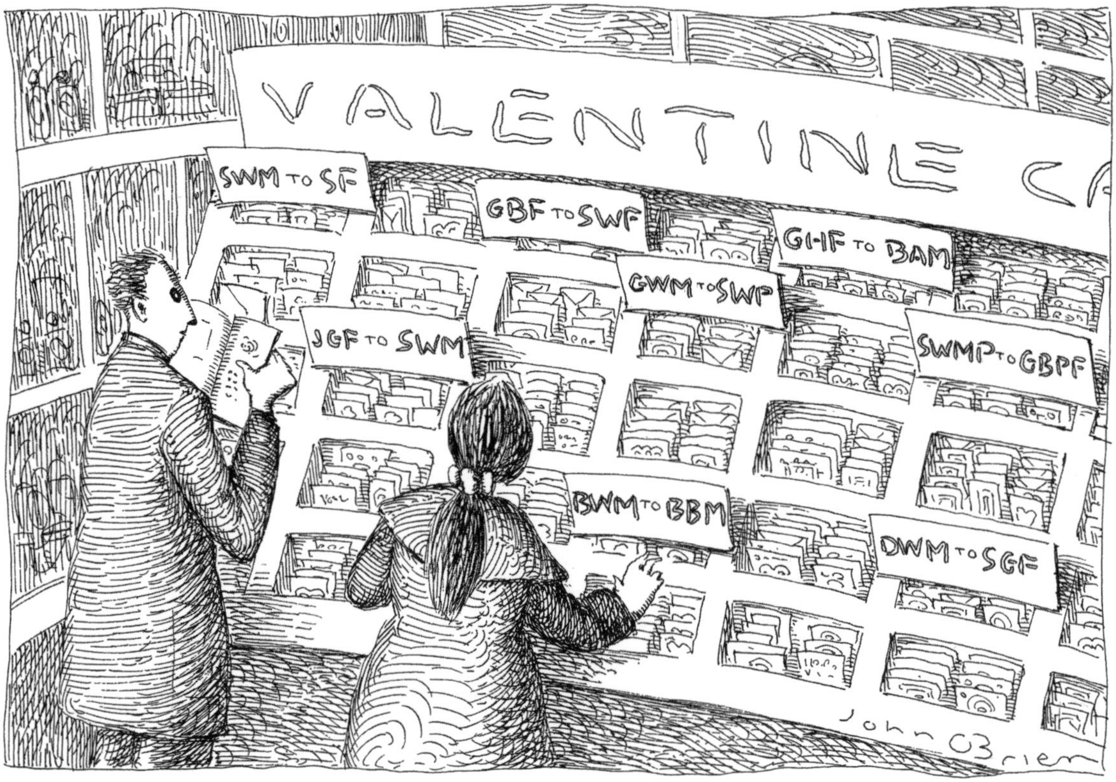
VALENTINE CA
SWM TO SF
GBF TO SWF
GHF TO BAM
GWM TO SWF
JGF TO SWM
SWMP TO GBPF
BWM TO BBM
DWM TO SGF
John O'Brien

eighteen"Think again, Muriel."

"Captions don't lie, Phil."

"I'm looking for a man who doesn't want anything to do with the wedding planning."

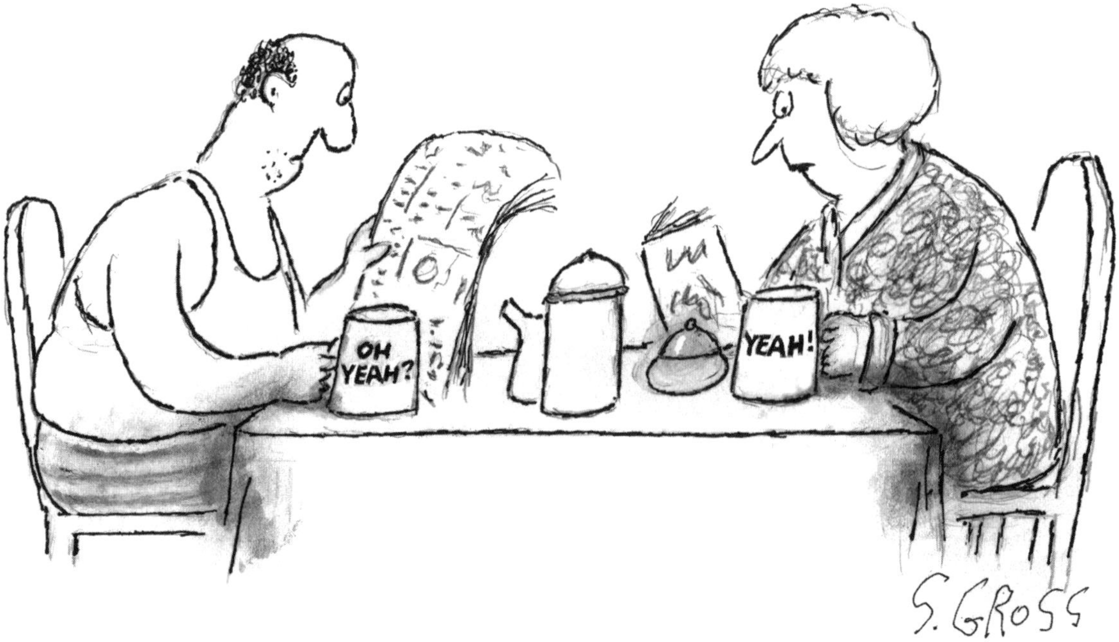
OH YEAH?
YEAH!
S. GROSS

"Richard and Sarah have written their own vows, God help us all."

"I love weddings. I'm going to have a bunch."

"We really need to talk about our relationship, so I've booked us on a TV show."

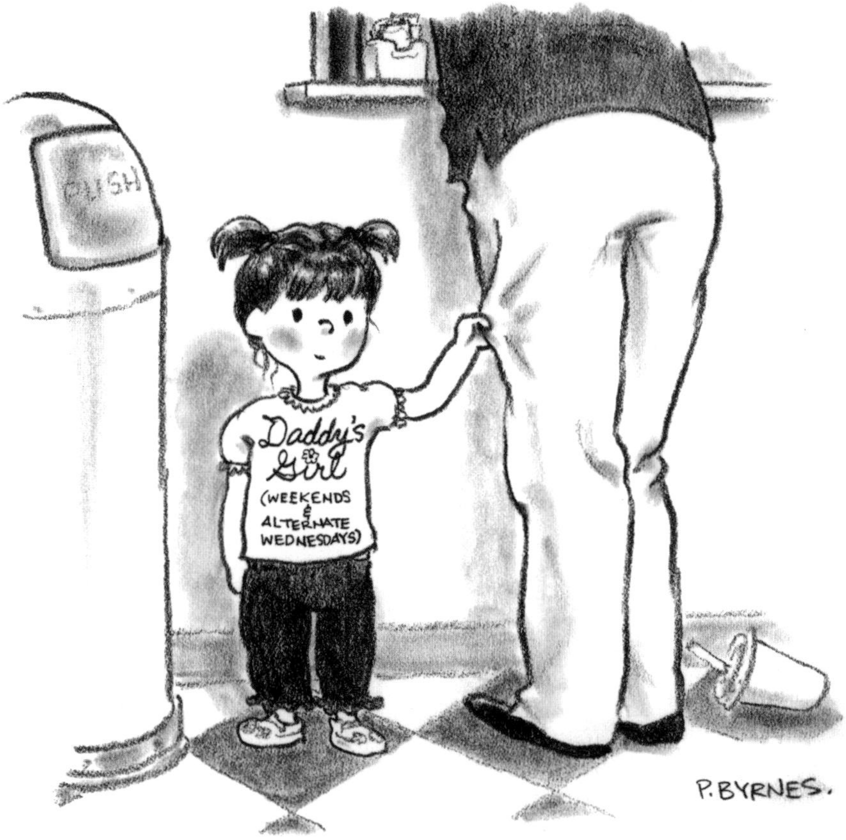
HSUP
Daddy's Girl
(WEEKENDS & ALTERNATE WEDNESDAYS)
P. BYRNES.

"First, I'll read the minutes from your last weddings."

"All right, I was wrong. A Shih Tzu was *not* all that was missing from our marriage."

"My wife! My best tie!"

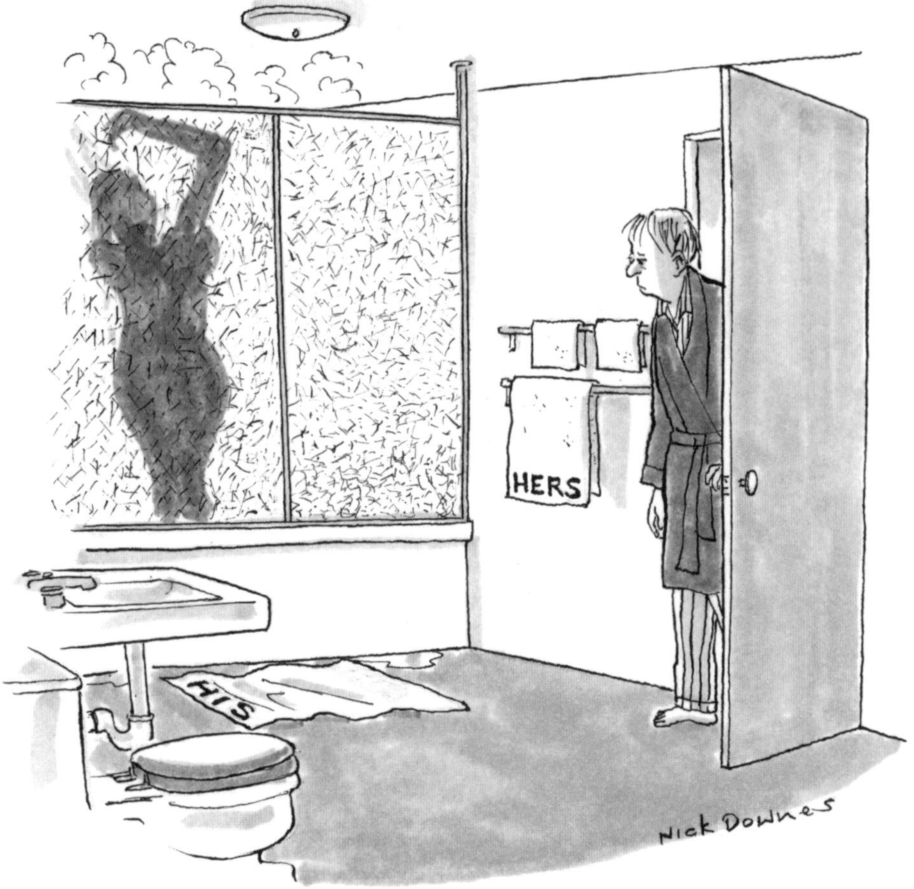
HERS
HIS
Nick Downes

"This is my last visit, Martha. I got the marriage posthumously annulled."

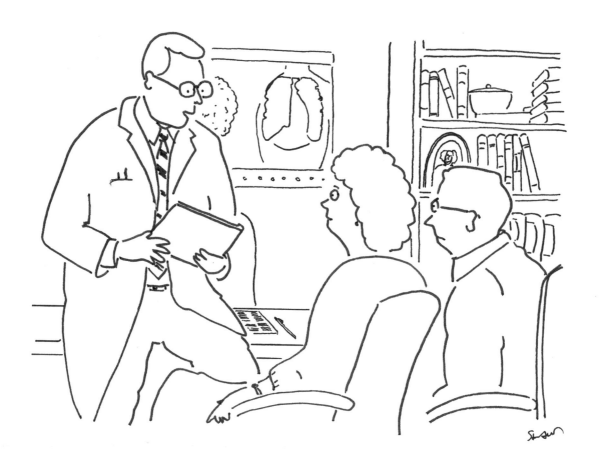

"I've identified that mysterious lump, Mrs. Feldman. It's your husband."

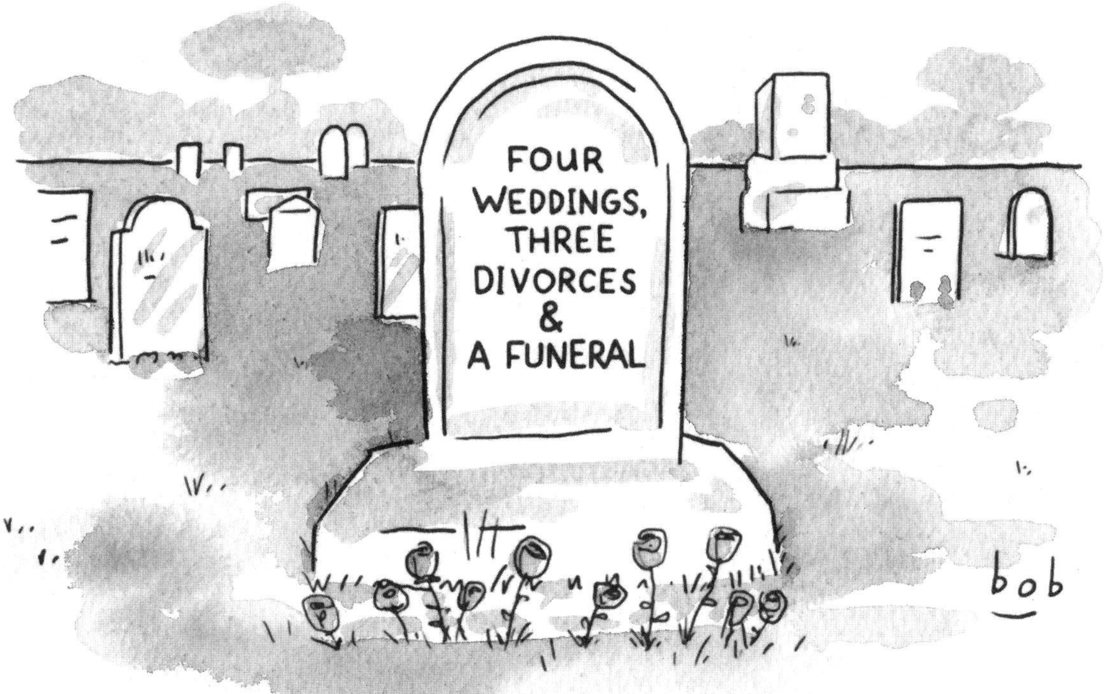
FOUR
WEDDINGS,
THREE
DIVORCES
&
A FUNERAL
bob

Contributors

Marisa Acocella (99) is a *New York Times* bestselling author, and her books include *Ann Tenna*, *Cancer Vixen*, and *Just Who the Hell is She, Anyway?* Her cartoons have appeared in the *New Yorker*, *O* magazine, *Glamour*, *W*, and the *New York Times*.

David Borchart (30) is a cartoonist for the *New Yorker*, and his cartoons have appeared in *Esquire* and *Time*.

Pat Byrnes (80, 103, 132), *New Yorker* cartoonist since 1998, won the National Cartoonists Society's Best Gag Cartoonist award in 2017. Previous careers include voice actor, ad copywriter, and aerospace engineer.

Roz Chast (52, 62, 114) is an award-winning *New Yorker* cartoonist and *New York Times* bestselling author. Her new book is *Going Into Town: A Love Letter to New York*.

Frank Cotham (39, 95) sold his first cartoon to the *New Yorker* in 1993. Since then he has sold over 750 cartoons to the magazine. His work can be seen at cartooncollections.com.

Matt Diffee (28, 79, 86, 111) is a cartoonist, among other things. His book *Hand Drawn Jokes for Smart Attractive People* isn't for everyone.

Liza Donnelly (105, 130) is an award-winning cartoonist and writer for the *New Yorker* and is resident cartoonist at CBS News. Donnelly's book *Women On Men* was a finalist for the Thurber Prize for American Humor, and her history of women cartoonists, *Funny Ladies: The New Yorker's Women Cartoonists*, is considered a resource for historians.

Nick Downes's (73, 87, 92, 136) work has appeared in many magazines in both the US and UK. He has had published two collections of his cartoons as well as a successful line of irreverent, rather subversive, greeting cards.

J. C. Duffy (40, 83, 125) has been a *New Yorker* cartoonist since 1998. In addition to cartooning and writing for other magazines, he also produces the long-running syndicated newspaper comic strip *The Fusco Brothers*.

Bob Eckstein (15, 48, 139) is editor of *The Ultimate Cartoon Book* series and a *New York Times* bestselling author. His work has appeared in *SPY*, *MAD*, *National Lampoon*, *Playboy*, and the *New Yorker*. He can be followed at bobeckstein.com and @Bob_Eckstein.

Liana Finck's (12, 66) work appears regularly in the *New Yorker*. Her most recent book is *Excuse Me*, published by Random House in 2019.

Mort Gerberg (97) is a cartoonist and author whose work has appeared in the *New Yorker*, *Playboy*, and many other magazines and newspapers, and on television, online, and in books. His *Cartooning: The Art and the Business* is considered the most comprehensive, authoritative book on the subject. His work can be found at mortgerberg.com.

Alex Gregory (19, 32, 38, 53, 57, 131) is a Hollywood screenwriter. His work can be seen on cartooncollections.com.

Sam Gross (11, 33, 59, 106, 128) has created around thirty thousand cartoons. He has published many cartoon books and was the cartoon editor for *National Lampoon*, *Smoke*, and *Parents* magazine.

William Haefeli's (9, 26, 34, 56, 61, 70, 91, 93, 112, 127) cartoons have been appearing in the *New Yorker* since 1998. He lives in Los Angeles.

Sid Harris (65, 78) has published thousands of cartoons. Many can be seen at sciencecartoonsplus.com. He has two new books: *Eureka! Cartoons on Chemistry* and *Damn Particles: Physics Cartoons*.

Trevor Hoey's (49) cartoons have appeared in the *New Yorker* since 2007. His cartoons can be seen at cartooncollections.com.

Amy Hwang (64) has been a cartoonist for the *New Yorker* since 2010. Her cartoons have also appeared in *Air Mail* and *EatingWell* and can be seen at amyhwang.com.

Bruce Eric Kaplan (25, 44, 55, 69, 82, 98, 121) is a cartoonist for the *New Yorker* and a television writer and producer.

Edward Koren (13, 18, 36, 47, 89) has contributed to the *New Yorker* since 1962. He has been a Guggenheim Fellow, and was Vermont's Cartoonist Laureate from 2015 to 2018.

Ken Krimstein (119) is a cartoonist, graphic novelist, writer, and 3.5-level tennis player. In 2018 he published *The Three Escapes of Hannah Arendt: A Tyranny of Truth*. You can see more of his work at kenkrimstein.com.

Robert Leighton (85, 94, 110, 120, 129) (robert-leighton.com) has been contributing to the *New Yorker* since 2002. As a puzzle-writer, he cowrote *The New Yorker Book of Cartoon Puzzles and Games*.

Arnie Levin (60, 135) is a cartoonist, illustrator, and animation director. His work can be seen at cartooncollections.com. Plus he is covered from head to toe in tattoos.

Bob Mankoff (10, 50, 109, 137) has published over 950 cartoons in the *New Yorker* magazine where he was cartoon editor for twenty years. He is now the cartoon editor at *Wired* and *Air Mail* magazine and president of cartooncollections.com.

Michael Maslin (45, 76, 88, 104, 134) began contributing to the *New Yorker* in 1977. His website, *Ink Spill*, is devoted to *New Yorker* cartoonists and cartoons.

Steve McGinn's (74) work appears regularly in *Funny Times* and has also appeared in *American Bystander* and *Weekly Humorist*. He was formerly the editorial page cartoonist at the *Beacon Hill Times*. His cartoons can be seen at cartooncollections.com and *Toons by Stev-o* and can be followed at *@toonsbystevo*.

Warren Miller (14, 23, 77) started selling cartoons to *Playboy* and the *New Yorker* in 1961. His work has also appeared in *Esquire*, *Punch*, *Rolling Stone*, *Audubon*, *Harvard Business Review*, *Barron's*, *Time*, *Newsweek*, and the *New York Times*. He has over 1,400 *New Yorker* cartoons.

Paul Noth (7, 81, 108, 133) is a staff cartoonist for the *New Yorker*, where his work has appeared regularly since 2004. He has written for *Late Night with Conan O'Brien* and been an animation consultant for *Saturday Night Live*. He is the author of the middle-grade novels *How to Sell Your Family to the Aliens* and *How to Properly Dispose of Planet Earth*. See his work at paulnoth.com.

John O'Brien's (8, 22, 68, 118, 124) work can be found in many publications including over one hundred children's books. He has done over two hundred cartoons and seventeen covers for the *New Yorker*. He can be found living in South Jersey or at johnobrienillustrator.com.

Teresa Burns Parkhurst's (113) cartoons have been published in a number of magazines, most recently the *New Yorker* and with several greeting card companies. She was counted among the Usual Gang of Idiots at *MAD* magazine from 2003 until 2019. She enjoys not going places.

Victoria Roberts (84) was born in New York City in 1957. Brought up in Mexico City and Sydney, Australia, Victoria became a cartoonist under contract to the *New Yorker* in 1987. Also a writer and performer, her show *Nona Appleby* will premiere in Sydney in 2021.

Danny Shanahan (27, 46, 51, 63, 96) has had more than 1,200 cartoons and a dozen covers published in the *New Yorker*, as well many other publications, including *Esquire*, *Fortune*, *Playboy*, and the *New York Times*. He has published four anthologies of his work and has appeared in dozens of *New Yorker* collections. He lives in Rhinebeck, New York.

Michael Shaw (16, 37, 42, 58, 116, 117, 122, 138) has slept in the attic at 77 Jefferson Ave, Columbus, Ohio, and may (or may not) have been bitten by the ghost of Muggs. His cartoons have appeared on *60 Minutes*, *Ronan Farrow Daily*, and cocktail napkins. Want to learn more? Google him!

Barbara Smaller's (31, 123) cartoons have appeared in numerous publications, anthologies, and, since 1996, regularly in the *New Yorker*. She is currently working on a book based on drawings from her Course of Empire series that has been featured in the *New Yorker*'s Daily Shouts.

Edward Steed (41) has been a cartoonist for the *New Yorker* since 2013.

Mick Stevens (17, 21, 67, 90) has been drawing cartoons for the *New Yorker* for over thirty-five years. His work has also appeared in many other publications, including *Narrative* magazine, *Air Mail*, *Wired*, *Barron's*, and *Harvard Business Review*. He has also illustrated several books, among them *Lobster Theory*. Examples of his work can be seen online, including on Instagram.

Julia Suits (54, 101) is a *New Yorker* cartoonist and freelance illustrator. She lives in Austin, Texas. To see more of her projects, visit juliasuits.net.

Larry Trepel's (100) work has appeared in the *New Yorker*, *National Lampoon*, and many other magazines. He currently has a monthly feature in *Sports Car Market* magazine.

P. C. Vey's (20, 43, 115) cartoons regularly appear in the *New Yorker*. His work also has been published in *Harvard Business Review*, *Barron's*, *National Lampoon*, the *Wall Street Journal*, the *New York Times*, *Prospect*, *Playboy*, *AARP Bulletin*, and the *Boston Globe*. He has three collections of cat cartoons and has contributed to many books of cartoons on a variety of subjects. For more go to pcvey.com.

Kim Warp (72) began contributing to the *New Yorker* in 1999 and is a winner of the National Cartoonists Society's Best Gag Cartoonist of the Year (2000). She frequently contributes the *New Yorker*'s Daily Cartoon.

Christopher Weyant (24, 35, 71, 75) is a cartoonist for the *New Yorker* and an editorial cartoonist for the *Boston Globe*. His picture book, *You Are (Not) Small*, won the Theodor Seuss Geisel Award. Follow him at christopherweyant.com and on Instagram @christopherweyant.

Jack Ziegler (29, 102, 107, 126) was a cartoonist for the *New Yorker* magazine from 1974 to 2017. During his lifetime he produced over 24,000 cartoons, and sold over 3,000, mainly to the *New Yorker*. You can find his work at jackziegler.com.

Acknowledgments

Thank you to all the contributing artists. Thank you Sam Gross for the wonderful cover. Thanks to Mitch Kaplan of Books & Books, everyone at the Cartoon Collections including Trevor Hoey, Bob Mankoff, Samantha Vuignier, and Jessica Ziegler. Thank you to Nicole Lowry and the Cartoon Bank. Thank you Michael Gerber and *American Bystander* for your support. Special thanks to my agent Joy Tutela.

And a big thank-you to Kristen, Rob, Wes, Jessica, Paul, Natalie, and the rest of the Princeton Architectural Press team.

—*Bob Eckstein*

Published by
Princeton Architectural Press
202 Warren Street
Hudson, New York 12534
www.papress.com

© 2021 Bob Eckstein
All rights reserved.
Printed and bound in China
24 23 22 21 4 3 2 1 First edition

ISBN: 978-1-61689-939-4

Editor: Kristen Hewitt
Series design: Paul Wagner
Design assistance: Natalie Snodgrass

Front cover: Sam Gross
Back cover: Mick Stevens

For permission to reprint cartoons, on pages listed, we gratefully thank the cartoonists and the following publications:

AirMail 139
Fantasy & Science Fiction 87
Narrative 119
New Yorker 7, 8, 9, 10, 11, 12, 13, 14, 16, 18, 19, 22, 23, 25, 26, 27, 28, 30, 32, 33, 34, 36, 38, 39, 41, 44, 46, 47, 49, 50, 51, 52, 53, 55, 57, 59, 60, 61, 63, 64, 66, 67, 69, 68, 71, 72, 77, 79, 82, 83, 84, 86, 89, 90, 91, 93, 95, 96, 98, 101, 109, 111, 112, 116, 118, 121, 123, 124, 127, 131, 132, 133, 134, 137
Notre Dame magazine 80
Parade 20
Punch 78
Rejection Collection 97, 108, 135
The Spectator 92, 136
Wall Street Journal 73

Library of Congress Control Number: 2020934726.